— HOW TO —
OVERCOME
CHILDHOOD TRAUMA

Break Free from the Pain of the Past—A Life-Changing Guide to Healing, Self-Love, and Emotional Freedom

by

DR. ELISE MONROE

How to Overcome Childhood Trauma :
Break Free from the Pain of the Past—A
Life-Changing Guide to Healing, Self-Love,
and Emotional Freedom

TABLE OF CONTENTS

Understanding the Roots of Your Childhood Pain
WHAT IS CHILDHOOD TRAUMA AND ITS LASTING EFFECTS

THE HIDDEN WOUNDS OF EMOTIONAL NEGLECT, ABUSE, AND ABANDONMENT

HOW CHILDHOOD TRAUMA SHAPES YOUR BRAIN, BODY, AND RELATIONSHIPS

SURVIVAL MODE PATTERNS YOU DIDN'T CHOOSE

Breaking Free from the Past
RECOGNIZING YOUR TRIGGERS AND CONNECTING WITH YOUR INNER CHILD

SETTING HEALTHY BOUNDARIES WITHOUT GUILT OR FEAR

RELEASING SHAME, GUILT, AND SELF-BLAME THAT HOLD YOU BACK

HEALING THE INNER CRITIC TO REBUILD SELF-WORTH

Reclaiming Emotional Freedom
THE POWER OF SELF-COMPASSION AND CULTIVATING SELF-LOVE

BEGINNING YOUR JOURNEY TO HEALING

Healing from childhood trauma is not a simple process, nor is it something that can be rushed. It's a deeply personal journey that requires courage, patience, and the willingness to confront pain that has often been buried for years. Whether you're someone who has lived with the invisible scars of early experiences or a professional or loved one supporting someone on this path, this book is designed to be a compassionate guide toward understanding and transforming that pain.

The wounds from childhood don't always show up in obvious ways. Sometimes, they lurk quietly beneath the surface—in the way you relate to others, the fears that unexpectedly overwhelm you, or in a persistent feeling of not quite being enough. These experiences shape more than just memories; they influence patterns of thinking, the ways we cope, and the foundation of our emotional world. This makes the journey to healing a bit like navigating a map with hidden landmarks. You know the territory is there, but it takes effort and guidance to find your way through it.

It's important to acknowledge that this journey isn't about blaming or reliving the past endlessly. Instead, it's centered on gaining clarity and reclaiming control over your life today. Healing means recognizing how past events still affect you and learning how to gently turn toward those feelings without being overwhelmed. It's about learning new ways to take care of yourself, shifting old patterns that no longer serve you, and discovering strength where you might have felt powerless.

One of the first steps in this process is understanding that you're not alone. Childhood trauma affects millions of people, cutting across all kinds of backgrounds, and many have found paths out of the weight of pain toward greater peace and resilience. This book is a companion on that path—a place where knowledge, empathy, and practical advice come together to empower you. It's designed to provide not only insights but actionable steps that you can take at your own pace.

Healing requires a gentle balance between awareness and self-compassion. Often, survivors of childhood trauma carry shame and self-criticism alongside their pain. So, you might expect to wrestle with those feelings as you explore your inner world. That's okay and more normal than you might think. The key is to meet yourself with kindness rather than judgment, allowing space for the parts of you that have been hurt. As you read through these pages, you'll find encouragement to embrace that compassion as a powerful tool in healing.

Every healing journey is unique, but many share common phases that we'll explore within this book. You'll encounter moments when progress feels slow or even nonexistent, and other times when breakthroughs arrive, bringing new hope. The path isn't linear. It bends and doubles back on itself, reflecting the complexity of the human experience. That's why it's vital to cultivate patience, understanding that healing is about growth and renewal, not perfection.

For those supporting survivors—whether as therapists, friends, or family members—this book offers insights to deepen your empathy and practical guidance to be more effective allies. Understanding the complexities of trauma helps to shift interactions toward support rather than frustration or avoidance. Healing does not happen in isolation, and nurturing relationships built on trust and safety plays an essential role in sustained recovery.

The journey ahead will invite you to explore difficult questions, face uncomfortable emotions, and shift long-held beliefs about yourself and your worth.

But within those challenges also lies tremendous opportunity. Healing opens the door to reclaiming parts of you that may have been lost or hidden—you're rediscovering your true essence beyond the pain. It's a process of transformation that can lead to a life filled with meaning, connection, and emotional freedom.

It's tempting to want quick fixes or easy answers, but healing demands more than that. It calls for respectful attention to the body and mind, and often the support of others who understand the complexity of trauma. This book encourages you to take your time, listen deep inside, and honor your feelings throughout this journey. It also equips you with tools and perspectives that promote empowerment rather than helplessness.

Most importantly, beginning your journey to healing means acknowledging your own inner strength. Even if trauma has shaped you in ways you didn't want, it hasn't defined your entire story. You have the ability to rewrite your future. The chapters ahead will guide you to understand where your pain comes from, learn to set boundaries that protect you, and develop practices that nurture your well-being.

While this is just the start, the decision to heal is itself an act of profound courage and self-love. It means choosing to step out of shadows into the possibility of light. This process might not be easy, but it's one of the most rewarding investments you can make—because your emotional freedom, peace, and happiness are worth it.

As you turn the pages, know that this book is crafted to meet you exactly where you are. It's not about rushing but about steady progress. Open your heart to the potential for growth and allow the insights here to support your journey. The path to healing is yours to walk, and this guide hopes to be a steady companion along the way.

CHAPTER 1

····•·■·•·■·•·■·•·■·◀◆▶·■·•·■·•·■·•·■·•·····

UNDERSTANDING THE ROOTS OF YOUR CHILDHOOD PAIN

Healing begins by shining a light on the origins of your childhood pain, recognizing that trauma isn't just about dramatic moments but often lives in the silent spaces of neglect, abandonment, or subtle emotional wounds that shaped how you see yourself and the world. These early experiences don't just fade with time; they rewire your brain, influence your body's reactions, and silently script patterns that govern your relationships and survival mechanisms. Acknowledging this truth isn't about blaming your past but about understanding the deep-rooted impact it's had so you can begin to reclaim control over your present. With awareness as the first step, you unlock the possibility of change by learning how these hidden injuries have influenced who you've become, empowering you to choose a path toward healing that feels both compassionate and courageous.

What Is Childhood Trauma and Its Lasting Effects

Childhood trauma is more than just a difficult experience; it's an event or series of events that overwhelm a child's ability to cope, shatter their sense of safety, and leave scars that can persist well into adulthood. It's important to recognize that trauma doesn't always stem from dramatic or violent incidents. Sometimes, the harm is subtle, creeping in through chronic neglect, emotional unavailability, or repeated invalidation. These experiences can undermine a child's basic trust in the world and in themselves.

When trauma strikes in childhood, it interrupts the natural flow of development. A child's brain is still rapidly forming, wiring itself based on experiences, especially those that carry strong emotional weight. Trauma distorts this wiring, reshaping brain circuits responsible for dealing with stress, processing emotions, and forming relationships. The rawness of this impact often leaves survivors feeling caught in patterns that seem impossible to escape, even decades later. This is why childhood trauma isn't something left behind in a dusty corner of the past—it lives in the body, the mind, and the heart.

The lasting effects of childhood trauma can be incredibly varied, affecting every aspect of a person's life. Some individuals develop anxiety, depression, or post-traumatic stress disorder (PTSD). Others struggle with emotional regulation, finding it hard to manage feelings of anger, sadness, or fear. For many, trauma manifests in repeated difficulties with trust and intimacy, creating barriers that complicate friendships, partnerships, and family relationships. The pain can surface in unhealthy coping strategies, such as substance abuse, self-sabotage, or dissociation from one's own experiences.

What makes childhood trauma especially challenging is its invisibility; this trauma doesn't always appear as cuts or bruises. Instead, it can look like shame, low self-esteem, or a persistent sense of not belonging. Many survivors have carried these wounds silently, not fully understanding why they feel "off" or why their reactions to everyday stress seem amplified. The lack of external validation often makes it harder to seek help because others might dismiss or misunderstand the depth of the pain.

One of the core reasons childhood trauma has such enduring effects is how it hijacks the brain's threat response system. When a child experiences trauma, their brain's alarm bells stay on high alert, primed to detect danger even when there isn't any. This chronic state of hypervigilance becomes a default mode that colors adult experiences. Moments of calm can feel unsafe, relationships may evoke fear instead of comfort, and minor conflicts can trigger overwhelming reactions. Even unconscious triggers, like certain smells or tones of voice, can bring the nervous system back to a traumatic state without warning.

Moreover, trauma disrupts the integration of memories. Unlike ordinary memories, which are stored in a coherent, narrative form that makes sense, traumatic memories can fragment and become lodged in the body or subconscious. This means that flashbacks, nightmares, or inexplicable emotional responses aren't random; they are the brain's way of trying to process overwhelming events that never fully made sense in the first place. These fragmented experiences can feel like the trauma is still happening, reinforcing a never-ending cycle of distress.

It's also crucial to understand that childhood trauma impacts identity. Children internalize the messages they receive from caregivers and the world around them. When those messages are tinged with fear, neglect, or abuse, children often grow up believing they are unworthy or fundamentally flawed. This internal narrative shapes how they see themselves and their place in the world. Healing begins with the awareness of this deep imprint and gently challenging those limiting beliefs.

For many survivors, the emotional landscape shaped by trauma is complex and contradictory. On one hand, there's a desperate quest for safety and connection; on the other, there's an instinctive withdrawal to avoid further pain. This push and pull makes relationships complicated and raises the risk of loneliness and isolation. Recognizing these patterns as trauma responses rather than character defects creates a powerful shift toward self-compassion.

It's also common to feel as if trauma has "stunted" some parts of development. For example, a person might find it hard to regulate emotions like an adult or struggle with trusting their own judgment. These developmental delays aren't signs of weakness but consequences of a brain and body that were forced to prioritize survival over growth at critical periods. Healing involves reclaiming these lost parts of ourselves and giving them the attention and nurturing they never received in childhood.

Importantly, childhood trauma's ripple effects extend beyond the individual. It influences families and communities, often perpetuating cycles of pain through generations. Patterns of behavior that emerge as survival mechanisms in one generation can unintentionally create challenges for the next. Understanding this dynamic helps break these cycles and inspires hope that healing is not only possible but can create a lasting impact that benefits future generations.

Physical health is another area where the effects of childhood trauma are profound. Chronic stress from trauma can influence everything from immune system functioning to heart health. People who've experienced trauma are more prone to illnesses such as autoimmune disorders, metabolic conditions, and chronic pain syndromes. Scientists are increasingly recognizing trauma as a significant factor in the mind-body connection, emphasizing that healing involves both psychological and physical care.

Despite the depth of childhood trauma's impact, there is a message of hope at the core of this understanding. Trauma survivors often carry remarkable resilience, a testimony to their strength even in the face of overwhelming adversity. The journey toward healing isn't about erasing the past but learning to live fully with it. It's about transforming pain into power, making sense of the chaos, and discovering new pathways to joy and connection.

Recognizing childhood trauma and its lasting effects is not a call to label or pathologize but an invitation to a compassionate understanding—both of ourselves and others. It's a step toward reclaiming a sense of agency and rewriting a story that may have been filled with silence, pain, and confusion. When we name the trauma and acknowledge its profound influence, we open the door to possibility—possibility for healing, for growth, and for a life defined by strength rather than suffering.

In the chapters that follow, we'll explore practical strategies and hearts-centered approaches to healing from childhood trauma. But first, it's essential to sit with the reality of what trauma means. To know what you're dealing with is the first spark of courage on this path. No one's journey is the same, but understanding these roots is the foundation for every hopeful step forward.

The Hidden Wounds of Emotional Neglect, Abuse, and Abandonment

When we talk about childhood trauma, the conversation often gravitates toward the more visible scars—physical abuse, for example, or overt neglect. But some of the deepest wounds aren't visible at all. Emotional neglect, abuse, and abandonment leave hidden marks that ripple through a person's inner world in ways that are subtle yet profound. These wounds shape the core of how you see yourself and the world, quietly undermining your sense of safety, worth, and belonging. Unlike physical injuries that heal and fade over time, emotional injuries are easily overlooked, misunderstood, and, sadly, often dismissed. Yet they hold immense power over your emotional life well into adulthood, affecting your relationships, self-image, and even your health.

Emotional neglect is a type of invisible injury that happens when a child's needs for love, attention, and validation aren't met—not because the caregivers were cruel, but often simply because they were overwhelmed, unavailable, or unable to provide what was needed. This absence of emotional nourishment leaves a child feeling unseen and unheard. It creates an aching void, a silent question: "Am I not worthy enough to be noticed or comforted?" This question, when left unanswered, can lead to a persistent feeling of emptiness or an internalized belief that one's feelings don't matter.

Abuse—whether emotional, verbal, or psychological—layered on top of neglect, compounds the damage. It sends a stark, damaging message: "You are not only unimportant, but you are also flawed, dangerous, or bad." These messages embed themselves in early neural pathways, wiring the brain to expect criticism, fear, or rejection rather than kindness or safety. Emotional abuse often involves constant criticism, manipulation, or humiliation, and unlike physical wounds, these types of scars are hard to identify, even for the person carrying them.

Then there's abandonment—the shock of being left behind, whether physically or emotionally. Sometimes abandonment is blatant, like a parent leaving or disappearing, but just as often, it's more subtle; it wears the mask of inconsistency, unpredictability, or emotional unavailability. The child learns to live without reliable support, grappling with the terrifying uncertainty of whether loved ones will stay or leave. This breeds anxiety and a hyper-vigilant mindset, where one is always braced for loss or betrayal.

These three forms of childhood trauma—emotional neglect, abuse, and abandonment—don't usually happen in isolation. They intertwine and support one another, creating a complex web of hurt that's difficult to disentangle. It's important to recognize that their impacts extend far beyond childhood, shaping the adult self in ways that feel automatic and unchangeable.

The hidden wounds often lead to a constant internal struggle between the parts of you that crave love and connection and those that fear vulnerability and rejection. You might find yourself withdrawing from others to avoid the pain of potential abandonment, or you might push people away preemptively, believing that if you hurt them first, you'll be spared. Trust can feel like an impossible gamble when you carry these wounds. Your heart wants connection, but your mind warily anticipates loss.

Many adults who have experienced these forms of trauma carry a strong sense of shame and self-blame. They blame themselves for not being enough to receive the love they needed, or for "causing" the neglect or abuse. This misplaced guilt builds walls around their true selves, preventing healing and acceptance. Shame thrives in silence and secrecy, often hidden not only from the outside world but also from the inner awareness of the individual. It's disguised as perfectionism, emotional numbness, or even self-sabotage.

Because these wounds are invisible, they make it difficult to articulate what went wrong. Sometimes it feels like there's a disconnect between your memories and your present emotions, resulting in confusion or numbness. You might sense something is "off" but struggle to explain it in words. This disconnect can be a form of emotional dissociation—a coping strategy developed in childhood to survive overwhelming pain.

But here's the key: recognizing and naming these hidden wounds is the first step in reclaiming your life. It's an act of courage and compassion to say, "What I experienced was real, and it affected me deeply." When emotional neglect and abuse stay silent, they have the power to control behavior and thought patterns in ways that feel uncontrollable. However, by shining a light on them, you begin to dismantle their hold.

Understanding these wounds doesn't mean dwelling endlessly on the past or getting stuck in victimhood. Instead, it offers a powerful foundation for healing—a way to start seeing yourself with more kindness and clarity. Emotional neglect teaches you how difficult it can be to ask for help, but realizing this opens up the possibility of learning how to meet your own needs or seek support from healthy relationships. Recognizing abuse's effects can help you identify toxic patterns in your adult relationships and choose to break free rather than repeat history.

The legacy of abandonment often manifests as an exaggerated need for reassurance or, conversely, as emotional distancing to avoid further hurt. When you understand this, you can work toward building internal stability and resilience, becoming the reliable presence your younger self needed but didn't have.

Healing is messy. It doesn't happen in a straight line. Sometimes progress feels like two steps forward and one step back, but every step is meaningful. The process requires patience because these wounds are entwined with your identity and survival strategies developed long ago. Undoing them means relearning how to trust yourself and others, how to feel safe within your own skin, and how to believe that you're deserving of love and care.

Therapeutic work often involves gently accessing these buried emotions, learning to sit with them without judgment, and building new neural pathways for emotional regulation and connection. It also means learning to re-parent yourself—to become the nurturing voice and steady presence that may have been missing in your childhood. This is not about replacing or blaming caregivers, but about reclaiming your power to heal and grow.

For those supporting survivors of emotional neglect, abuse, and abandonment, compassion and patience are vital. It's easy to underestimate the depth of invisible wounds and the courage it takes to confront them. Healing requires a safe space where vulnerability is honored, not dismissed. Even small acts of kindness and validation can help rebuild shattered self-worth.

In the end, understanding the hidden wounds opens the door to hope. It validates your pain while also emphasizing your capacity to heal. You are not doomed to carry these old injuries into the future; you can transform your relationship with your past, and in doing so, create a new narrative—one of resilience, love, and possibility. The scars may remain as reminders, but they don't have to define the rest of your story.

How Childhood Trauma Shapes Your Brain, Body, and Relationships

Childhood trauma doesn't just leave emotional scars; it rewires how your brain develops, how your body reacts to stress, and how you interact with the people around you. When you experience trauma early in life—whether through neglect, abuse, or abandonment—it activates survival mechanisms that prioritize immediate safety over long-term growth.

These changes can become embedded in your biology and behavior, often without your conscious awareness.

Neuroscience has shown how profoundly trauma affects the brain's architecture. The developing brain is like soft clay, highly sensitive to the environment it grows in. When trauma occurs, it can alter the way certain brain regions communicate and function. For instance, areas involved in processing emotions, like the amygdala and hippocampus, tend to become overactive or underdeveloped. This can make you highly reactive to perceived threats or cause difficulties in regulating emotions. You might find yourself easily overwhelmed, stuck in anxiety, or disconnected from your feelings, even long after the trauma is over.

Equally important is the effect trauma has on your body. Children who grow up in unsafe or chaotic environments often live in a state of chronic stress. This stress becomes a default "on" switch for the body's fight, flight, or freeze response. Over time, this state wears down the nervous system and can lead to what experts call "toxic stress." This kind of stress isn't just a mental burden—it's physically altering. It can change hormone levels, immune function, and even the way your body responds to pain or illness in adulthood. You might notice symptoms like chronic fatigue, muscle tension, or gastrointestinal problems that don't have an obvious medical cause. These physical reactions are your body's way of holding onto trauma, signaling that somewhere inside, distress remains unresolved.

Trauma also casts long shadows on relationships. Since early bonds with caregivers shape our blueprint for trust and attachment, disruptions here have real consequences. If your caregivers were emotionally unavailable, inconsistent, or harmful, your brain learned to protect itself by expecting pain or rejection. This deeply ingrained expectation shapes how you see others and yourself. You might find it hard to fully trust people or feel safe in close relationships. Sometimes, you push others away before they get too close, fearing abandonment. Other times, you cling tightly, terrified of losing connection. Either way, trauma programs relational patterns that repeat themselves in adulthood, even when you long for authentic connection and love.

Another subtle but powerful way trauma shapes you is through the internal "scripts" you adopt. These are self-defeating beliefs that develop as survival strategies during childhood. You might believe you're unlovable, broken, or responsible for the pain around you—but these ideas come from trauma's lens, not the truth of who you are. They influence every interaction, coloring your experiences and often reinforcing isolation or shame. Recognizing that these beliefs stem from adaptation rather than fact is a crucial step toward healing.

It's important to acknowledge the complexity of these effects without reducing your experience to a diagnosis. Trauma's imprint on your brain, body, and relationships is not a permanent sentence. The brain's natural plasticity means it can grow new pathways and heal with intentional effort and support. Likewise, your body can begin to release held tension and retrain responses through somatic work and mindful practices. Relationships can transform too, as you develop new ways of connecting rooted in safety and honesty.

Understanding these deep connections between trauma and your mind and body is not about labeling yourself as damaged. Instead, it's about reclaiming your story with compassion and clarity. Trauma shaped you once to protect you, but those strategies may no longer serve you as an adult. Learning this allows you to choose new ways of experiencing the world—ways that promote growth rather than just survival.

Many who have endured trauma find that simply knowing the "why" behind their reactions is incredibly freeing. When emotional flashbacks or physical symptoms arise, realizing they're tied to childhood experiences can create space for self-kindness rather than frustration. For example, the overwhelming anxiety before a simple social event isn't a personal failure; it's your nervous system responding as it did when you were unsafe as a child. This understanding reduces self-blame and opens a path toward change.

Still, peeling back the layers of trauma's impact can feel overwhelming. You may question if you'll ever feel truly stable or capable of healthy relationships. The truth is that healing isn't linear, and it requires patience. Your brain and body are remarkably resilient, but they also carry deep imprints that need gentle, sustained attention. Building this new foundation often means relearning how to trust your own body signals and emotions, which trauma usually disconnects you from.

One of the hardest but most essential parts of this journey is recognizing that the challenges in relationships aren't due to personal flaws. Trauma skews your expectations and reactions, making even safe situations feel unsafe. This can trap you in a cycle of loneliness or conflict that feels impossible to break. But by identifying these patterns as trauma responses rather than character weaknesses, you empower yourself to seek support and adopt healthier relational strategies.

When trauma shapes your brain and body, it can also affect your ability to regulate stress and emotions. You might experience mood swings, heightened irritability, or emotional numbness. These responses are your survival mechanisms turned against you now, reacting to everyday challenges with disproportionate intensity or shutting down completely. This is why grounding techniques, mindfulness, and therapeutic interventions that focus on body awareness often become central in healing trauma. They teach you how to calm your nervous system and reconnect to the present moment, where you are safe.

Additionally, trauma's imprint on your brain's reward system can affect your motivation and ability to experience joy. Many survivors struggle with feelings of emptiness or chronic dissatisfaction, even when life appears stable. This is partly because the brain's pathways for pleasure and reward can become blunted through prolonged stress. Recognizing that these feelings have biological roots—and are not a reflection of your worth—can reduce feelings of shame and highlight the importance of self-care in recovery.

As adults, we sometimes forget how much of our early environment still lives under the surface. The brain conserves energy by defaulting to the familiar, so old trauma patterns often resurface during times of stress or change. This explains why setbacks are common in healing but don't mean failure. Instead, they're reminders of where your wound exists and where your attention is needed. Trauma doesn't have to define you, but it does need to be understood and worked with, not ignored.

Your body holds memories that the mind may not fully grasp, and your relationships reflect internal dynamics shaped long ago. By exploring this interconnectedness, you start to dismantle the silent hold trauma keeps on your life. This work involves courage, because it means facing pain and vulnerability, but it also invites transformation and hope.

In the next chapters, you'll discover ways to recognize these trauma imprints in your daily life, tools to help you regulate your nervous system, and strategies to build healthier connections. Knowing how childhood trauma shaped your brain, body, and relationships creates a foundation for intentional healing—one where you reclaim your power at every level, and build the life you were always meant to live.

Survival Mode Patterns You Didn't Choose

When you reflect on your childhood pain, it's important to recognize that many of the behaviors you developed back then weren't conscious choices—they were survival tactics. These patterns, often ingrained deeply in your psyche and nervous system, emerged not because you wanted to adopt them but because they were the only ways you could navigate a world that felt unsafe, unpredictable, or even harmful. Survival mode doesn't come with a user manual. Instead, it imposes instincts and coping mechanisms that often stay with you long after the threats have passed.

Think back to those moments when you felt overwhelmed or threatened as a child. Your brain, wired to protect you at all costs, shifted gears into automatic responses designed to preserve safety:

freeze, fight, flight, or appease. These reflexes may have saved your life or at least kept emotional devastation at bay. But as the years tick by, these once vital strategies can morph into rigid patterns that limit your freedom, keep you stuck in old wounds, and sabotage your adult relationships.

It's crucial to understand that none of these survival mechanisms were your fault. You didn't wake up one day deciding to become hypervigilant, emotionally distant, or people-pleasing. Instead, your responses were adaptations—your mind and body's way of saying, "I will do whatever it takes to get through this." In other words, these so-called "patterns" weren't the choices you made; they were the choices your system made for you.

Survival mode often manifests through a range of behaviors that might seem self-destructive or confusing on the surface but make a lot more sense when seen through the lens of trauma. You might find yourself constantly scanning for danger in relationships, unable to trust others fully. Or maybe you react to criticism with overwhelming shame or defensiveness because, as a child, criticism felt like a direct threat to your very existence. These responses, although painful now, were once essential shields.

In some cases, survival looks like shutting down emotionally to avoid feeling hurt. This numbness acts like a buffer against relentless pain, giving you a break from overwhelming feelings that you didn't have the tools to manage as a child. Over time, this detachment can lead to a sense of emptiness or disconnection from yourself and others. Yet trying to feel anything else might have seemed too risky, too vulnerable.

Others might recognize familiar patterns of people-pleasing or perfectionism embedded in their survival strategies. These behaviors may have been ways to gain love, approval, or simply avoid punishment. Achieving "good enough" as a child often meant safety—for example, obeying a parent to escape verbal abuse or fulfilling impossible standards to prevent rejection. Though well-intentioned and adaptive in their original context, these behaviors can exhaust your spirit when carried unchecked into adulthood.

On the flip side, some individuals respond to survival mode with anger, mistrust, or withdrawal. If your environment forced you into constant hyper-alertness, you may have learned to anticipate harm from others, leading to defensive walls that keep people at a distance. This self-protection can be isolating, but in the moment, it probably felt like the only way to survive.

Because these survival patterns developed early, they often feel like an inseparable part of your identity. This can create a challenging paradox: on one hand, these behaviors helped you endure trauma; on the other, they might be the very things preventing your healing and growth now. Recognizing this internal conflict is the first step toward compassion—not only for your past self but for the ways you've been trying to cope.

It's also common to minimize or dismiss these survival patterns because they're so ingrained. You might believe that if you just "try harder" or "be stronger," these behaviors will naturally fall away. Unfortunately, survival responses are deeply rooted in the nervous system and emotional memory, making them resistant to quick fixes or sheer willpower. Healing demands patience, self-awareness, and sometimes guidance to help your system learn new ways to respond.

In many ways, survival mode behaviors resemble a double-edged sword. They were necessary adaptations that shaped how you navigated danger, but they also create barriers to feeling safe and joyful in adulthood. These patterns interfere with vulnerability, intimacy, and self-expression. They may lead you to make choices that perpetuate patterns of pain without realizing it. Understanding this helps you become an active participant in your healing journey rather than remaining stuck in unconscious cycles.

Meeting your survival mode patterns with empathy is a radical act. It shifts the narrative away from blame and toward understanding why you did what you had to do. This perspective is empowering because it affirms that you were resourceful, even if those resources no longer serve your current life.

From here, the path forward involves gently unraveling these survival patterns and asking yourself, "What did this protect me from? Is this pattern still protecting me today or holding me back?" It's a slow process, often requiring you to retrain your nervous system and challenge long-held beliefs about yourself and the world.

When you start to disarm these survival behaviors, you also create space to discover the parts of you that were hidden—your true self that has been waiting for safety and acceptance. This is the self that can begin to heal, create new boundaries, and cultivate relationships based on mutual respect and trust. You don't have to carry the weight of survival mode forever.

There's no shame in recognizing that your early coping mechanisms were necessary adaptations. They served their purpose in an unsafe world. But healing means inviting curiosity about these patterns and understanding the ways they connect to your childhood experiences. It means nurturing self-compassion and allowing yourself the grace to unlearn survival mode, one step at a time.

It's within this space of awareness that transformation happens. You begin to reclaim agency over your reactions and beliefs. You start to see yourself as more than a survivor—you become a person with the capacity to thrive. This process is not linear, nor does it happen quickly, but it's deeply worthwhile. You deserve to live beyond survival, not bound by the chains of a past you didn't choose.

Survival mode patterns are a testament to your resilience. By understanding them fully, you turn the painful past into a foundation for strength instead of limitation. This awareness lays the groundwork for the next steps in your journey—stepping out of these patterns and embracing freedom, healing, and growth.

CHAPTER 2

BREAKING FREE FROM
THE PAST

Letting go of the grip childhood trauma holds isn't about erasing the past or pretending those wounds never happened—it's about reclaiming your power to choose how that past shapes your present. It starts with the brave act of recognizing the patterns that keep you stuck, the familiar reactions that aren't really yours but survival habits handed down from pain. This chapter invites you to gently confront those moments without judgment, to understand that breaking free means creating space to heal, not submitting to old narratives of guilt or shame. You'll begin to see that freedom comes from setting clear boundaries with your history and the people around you, and from nurturing the parts of yourself that were once silenced. In doing so, the insecurities and self-doubt that held you captive begin to loosen, paving the way for a life that's not defined by what happened, but by the strength and hope you carry forward.

Recognizing Your Triggers and Connecting with Your Inner Child

One of the most important steps in breaking free from the past is understanding what triggers you. Triggers are like emotional landmines buried deep in your heart and mind—unexpected, intense reactions to seemingly ordinary events that pull you back into the pain of childhood trauma. These reactions can feel overwhelming and confusing, especially when they show up without warning. They often surface as anger, sadness, anxiety, or even numbness, but beneath these feelings lies a message from your inner child, asking to be seen and heard.

Triggers are not random; they're connected to the wounds you carry from your earliest experiences. For example, you might feel abandoned when someone cancels plans last minute, echoing past feelings of neglect. Or, a harsh comment from a coworker might send you spiraling into intense self-doubt, resurfacing childhood moments where you were told you weren't good enough. Recognizing these triggers means paying close attention to what situations or words tend to ignite strong emotional responses within you. It's less about the event itself and more about the meaning you've attached to it because of past pain.

Connecting with your inner child is a powerful part of this process. This concept might sound abstract or even a little strange at first—thinking of yourself as the child you once were—but it's a transformative practice of reaching out tenderness and understanding to the part of you that still holds those childhood hurts and unmet needs. Your inner child is a vulnerable, emotional self that carries memories of both pain and innocence. She or he is waiting to be nurtured, comforted, and validated, just like any child would in a safe environment.

When you recognize a trigger, you're given an opportunity to pause and ask, "What part of me is reacting right now? What does my inner child feel in this moment?" This kind of self-inquiry allows you to step out of the immediate flood of emotions and gently observe what's happening inside. Instead of reacting in survival mode, which often leads to shutting down or lashing out, you create a space where healing can begin. It's as if you're turning on a light in a dark room, giving yourself the chance to understand the fear or pain that's been lurking in the shadows for so long.

This doesn't come easily. Many adults who've experienced childhood trauma were taught to ignore or suppress their feelings—to be "tough" or "self-reliant" because vulnerability seemed unsafe or shameful. But reconnecting with your inner child means allowing yourself to feel again, to grieve, to scream, or just to sit quietly with those feelings without judgment. It's about validating your pain rather than pushing it away. It's about telling that younger you she was not alone then, and she's not alone now.

When you start to recognize triggers and engage with your inner child, you might notice patterns in how these trigger responses show up. Maybe you get avoidant in relationships when things get intense. Or perhaps you have a tendency to overwork yourself to cover up feelings of worthlessness rooted in your past. These patterns don't make you broken—they make you human. And they offer clues that there's an unresolved part of your inner child seeking attention and healing.

Understanding triggers also helps you reclaim control. Trauma often robs people of that sense of control, making you feel helpless when memories or emotions flood your mind. But by noticing these emotional flashpoints early, you empower yourself to respond differently—perhaps by grounding yourself with deep breaths, talking to a trusted friend, or reminding your inner child that she's safe right now. These grounding techniques become tools for altering the way your brain and body react to distress.

Connecting with your inner child invites emotional honesty and compassion. The words you speak, both aloud and in your mind, should be gentle.

You might say, "I see you're hurting," or "It's okay to feel scared," as if comforting a real child. This practice can be incredibly healing because it rewrites the silent narrative many survivors hold—that their feelings don't matter or that their pain is a sign of weakness. Instead, nurturing your inner child affirms your experience and your worthiness of love and care.

There's also a sense of reclaiming the joy and creativity your inner child represents. Trauma can dim or even erase parts of that natural exuberance, leaving you feeling disconnected from yourself and the world. When you intentionally connect with your inner child, you open the door again to curiosity, playfulness, and wonder. These qualities don't disappear just because you suffered—they've just been buried under layers of survival and protection.

Engaging with this younger part of yourself can sometimes bring up resistance or fear. You might worry that confronting these feelings will make the pain worse or that others won't understand. These reactions are normal and deserve kindness rather than judgment. It helps to remember that healing isn't about erasing the past but learning to carry it with less suffering and more peace. Step by step, you're building a relationship with your inner child that offers safety and acceptance.

For mental health professionals and loved ones supporting survivors, recognizing triggers and the process of connecting with the inner child is a critical piece of compassionate care. It requires patience and sensitivity to witness someone's raw emotions and to offer validation without pushing too hard. Encouraging those healing to slow down and acknowledge their triggers invites profound releases and breakthroughs that can pave the way for lasting change.

In practical terms, keeping a journal of trigger moments and the feelings they evoke can be helpful. This awakening to patterns builds self-awareness, a core aspect of healing. You may also create gentle rituals or dialogues with your inner child—whether through writing letters, visualizations, or simply mindful breathing—to deepen this connection over time.

Recognizing your triggers and connecting with your inner child ultimately breaks the cycle of pain by shifting the relationship you have with your past. Instead of being controlled by unconscious memories and fears, you become an active participant in your healing journey. You learn to listen deeply, respond with kindness, and cultivate an internal world where that vulnerable child feels safe enough to grow.

This work is about more than avoiding pain. It's about reclaiming your own emotional freedom and discovering a resilience you may have thought was lost. When you embrace your triggers as gateways rather than enemies, and when you hold your inner child tenderly, the past begins to lose its power to define your present. This is the beginning of a new way to live—

one where your childhood no longer controls you, but where you control your healing.

Setting Healthy Boundaries Without Guilt or Fear

Breaking free from the past means reclaiming control over your life in a way that honors your needs and feelings. One of the most powerful tools in this process is setting healthy boundaries. Unfortunately, for many who've experienced childhood trauma, the concept of boundaries is tangled up with guilt, fear, and confusion. When boundaries weren't respected—or maybe they didn't exist at all in early life—it becomes difficult to believe you have the right to enforce them now. But it's essential to recognize that boundaries aren't walls built to keep others out; they are bridges drawn to protect your well-being and create respectful connections.

Setting boundaries is a radical act of self-respect. It tells you and those around you that your experiences, emotions, and limits matter. Trauma often teaches us to minimize our needs or to worry about disappointing others, because survival depended on those dynamics. As a result, you might feel anxious or selfish when trying to set limits, fearing rejection or conflict. However, the truth is, boundaries are an emotional compass that guides healthy relationships and self-care.

It's normal to feel resistance when you first start identifying and expressing your boundaries. You may hear that old inner critic whispering, "You're asking too much," or "You don't deserve this." These voices often carry the weight of outdated programming from your childhood. Learning to distinguish between your authentic self's voice and these inherited fears is key. A helpful step is to start small—practice saying no to minor requests and observe how it feels. Does your anxiety spike? Do you notice relief or empowerment? These moments are rich learning opportunities to recalibrate how you approach limits.

Boundaries can take many forms. Sometimes they're physical, like needing personal space; other times, they're emotional, such as not tolerating harsh criticism or dismissive behavior. Verbal boundaries might involve choosing the topics you want to discuss or how others speak to you. Whatever shape they take, boundaries are about defining what's safe and nourishing for you. This is especially vital for those healing from childhood trauma since early experiences often blurred or erased these lines completely.

When practicing boundary-setting, remember: you're not responsible for other people's reactions. It's easy to fall into the trap of policing others' feelings, especially if you grew up in unpredictable or invalidating environments. But your peace of mind and emotional safety come first. Clear boundaries actually empower better relationships because they foster honesty and respect. Without boundaries, resentment and confusion build, feeding patterns similar to those you are trying to leave behind.

One challenge you may encounter is feeling guilty for insisting on your limits, especially if boundary violations involve family or longtime friends. This guilt often stems from feeling indebted or loyal in ways that sacrifice your well-being. It helps to remind yourself that loyalty does not mean self-neglect. Healthy connection thrives on mutual respect—not on sacrificing your health for the sake of another person's comfort. Saying no or asking for space doesn't make you unloving or disloyal; it's a courageous step toward healthier, more balanced relationships.

Fear can show up as well, making it seem safer to stay silent rather than risk confrontation. Fear of abandonment, rejection, or conflict is deeply ingrained in many trauma survivors. The truth is, avoiding boundaries rarely prevents these outcomes in the long run—it often guarantees emotional exhaustion and deeper wounds. Setting boundaries doesn't guarantee that everyone will be pleased, but it ensures that you're honoring your truth, even if it feels uncomfortable at first. Over time, these actions build confidence and a stronger sense of self.

Practically speaking, setting healthy boundaries starts with self-awareness. Take time to reflect on your feelings during and after interactions. Notice where you felt drained, disrespected, or uneasy. Those feelings are signals that a boundary needs to be set or reinforced. Write them down if it helps—it clarifies what you need to say when the time comes. Communicating boundaries doesn't have to be elaborate or confrontational. Simple, direct statements like "I need some time to myself right now," or "I'm not comfortable talking about that," can be surprisingly effective.

Sometimes, you might worry you won't be able to maintain these boundaries, especially in relationships that have long histories of unhealthy dynamics. Keep in mind that boundaries are an ongoing process. They can be flexible and adjust as you grow. There may be setbacks or pushback, and that's part of the journey. Each time you reaffirm your limits, you reinforce your inner strength and resilience. Imagine it like building a muscle—consistency over time makes it stronger and easier to hold.

Another important aspect is learning to recognize the difference between genuine connection and people-pleasing. Trauma can intertwine your identity with the need to keep others happy or safe at your expense. Boundary-setting helps untangle this, allowing you to engage authentically rather than out of obligation or fear. This shift often attracts healthier, more reciprocal relationships and reduces the pain of emotional exhaustion and resentment.

Therapists, support groups, and mental health professionals can play a vital role in this work by providing a safe space to practice and validate your boundary-setting efforts. Sometimes having an external witness who understands your history strengthens your confidence. If you support someone healing from trauma, remember that encouraging their boundaries without judgment is one of the most powerful ways to show love. It's okay if that means recalibrating the relationship dynamic to respect their healing needs.

It's worth emphasizing that this process isn't about building walls that shut others out. Instead, boundaries invite you to show up as your most authentic self. They foster mutual respect, clarity, and emotional safety, which are essential to healing wounds from the past. Saying "no" or "I need X" gives you greater freedom and clarity to choose the relationships and experiences that truly support your recovery and growth.

Ultimately, setting healthy boundaries without guilt or fear is transformative. It rewires the old survival patterns that kept you stuck and replaces them with a foundation of self-respect and empowerment. This act of courage creates space for your inner child to feel safe and valued, fostering the healing and wholeness you deserve. Boundaries are a language of love—spoken first to yourself and then shared with the world in your own time and way.

Releasing Shame, Guilt, and Self-Blame That Hold You Back

One of the heaviest chains that keep many adults trapped in their childhood trauma is the weight of shame, guilt, and self-blame. These emotions can quietly infiltrate our minds and hearts, convincing us that we are responsible for the pain we endured or that we somehow deserved it. Holding on to these feelings drains energy, erodes self-esteem, and blocks the way to healing. The first step toward breaking free is understanding that these emotions, however powerful and persistent, are not truths but patterns learned under the harshest conditions.

Shame is especially pernicious because it wounds our sense of self. It tells us that we are inherently flawed, unworthy of love or belonging. Its voice is so loud and consistent that it can drown out our inner wisdom and kindness. Shame festers in secrecy, preferring isolation and silence. When you've grown up in an environment where your feelings or experiences were dismissed or invalidated, shame becomes the default lens through which you view yourself. It whispers lies, making you believe you are broken beyond repair.

Yet, shame thrives on misunderstanding. When you begin to recognize that shame is an emotional wound—an outdated protective mechanism rather than a reflection of your true worth—it loses some of its power. This shift isn't about denying painful feelings or pretending they don't exist. Instead, it's about recognizing shame as a story you were told, not a fact you have to live by. It means acknowledging those feelings with compassion and curiosity rather than judgment.

Guilt, closely related yet distinct from shame, often arises from misplaced responsibility. When childhood trauma occurs, especially in abusive or neglectful circumstances, children are often made to feel that they caused the pain or deserved the punishment. This internalized guilt becomes a persistent companion. Even as an adult, you might carry the sense that you should have done things differently or that you somehow failed to prevent what happened to you.

When guilt turns inward as self-blame, it becomes a toxic force that drains hope for healing. It's important to understand that guilt, in the context of trauma, is frequently unfairly assigned. You couldn't control the actions or mood swings of the adults around you, no matter how much you tried. The burden of guilt belongs with those who caused harm, not with you. This realization can be a turning point in the healing journey because it demands a reassessment of where responsibility truly lies.

Releasing shame, guilt, and self-blame doesn't happen overnight or through sheer willpower alone. It requires a willingness to sit with discomfort and to challenge internalized narratives through reflection and self-compassion. For many, this means confronting the inner critic—that relentless voice that amplifies shame and guilt—and replacing its messages with truths founded in kindness and reality. Remember, you are not your trauma, nor are you the mistakes or misconceptions you once believed.

What helps most in this process is reclaiming your narrative, understanding that childhood experiences do not define your worth or dictate your future. You are allowed to separate your identity from what was done to you. This separation is a courageous act that acknowledges pain without letting it rule. It invites you to become an ally to your own healing, to speak kindly to yourself when accusations arise, and to nurture your resilience with patience and understanding.

The journey at times can be lonely and fraught with resistance, especially if you've been told or made to feel that you should just 'get over it' or 'move on.' Healing shame and guilt means rejecting those harmful messages and creating a safe container where your emotions can be explored without condemnation. This might involve journaling, talking with trusted friends or therapists, or engaging in practices that ground you in present reality rather than past trauma.

Imagine your shame, guilt, and self-blame as shadows cast by an old, dim light. They lose their shape and size when exposed to the bright light of awareness and self-acceptance. Recognizing that these feelings were survival strategies meant to protect you during chaotic or unsafe times offers a new perspective. You weren't weak or defective for feeling them; you were human, adapting in a world that didn't give you choice or refuge.

Moreover, releasing these emotions creates space for other, more nurturing feelings to grow—like self-respect, hope, and empowerment. It doesn't mean you forget your past or the pain endured. Instead, it means you no longer let those emotions hold you hostage. As this space opens, you might notice how much more energy and clarity appear, how your relationships can shift when you're not weighed down by internal punishment, and how your vision for the future broadens.

In practical terms, this release might look like naming your shame and guilt in safe environments and recognizing moments when they arise in your daily life. Over time, you can catch those automatic feelings and question their validity. "Am I really responsible for this?" "Is this thought about myself true, or is it something I learned long ago?" Developing this habit of gentle inquiry empowers you to disrupt the emotional patterns that have held so tightly.

It's also important to acknowledge that self-blame can sometimes disguise itself as a misguided form of control—believing that if you just take responsibility, you can prevent future harm. While understandable, this belief can trap you in a cycle of blame that's impossible to break on your own. Healing requires learning to trust that safety and wellbeing come not from self-punishment but from self-care and boundaries that protect you now.

For the professionals and loved ones supporting survivors, it's crucial to hold a nonjudgmental, validating presence. Those recovering from trauma often get stuck in shame loops because their support systems once failed them or blamed them unfairly. Offering consistent empathy and reinforcing the message that trauma is not the survivor's fault can help untangle these persistent feelings.

Ultimately, releasing shame, guilt, and self-blame is about reclaiming your humanity and your right to heal. It's a radical act of kindness and courage to look inward and decide that you deserve compassion, no matter what. While the past can't be rewritten, your relationship with it can transform. Instead of carrying shame and guilt as lifelong baggage, you can choose to set them down, moving forward with a lighter heart and a clearer path toward emotional freedom.

Remember, the process isn't linear. Some days might feel like progress, while others may pull you back into old patterns. That's part of the journey. Each moment you choose understanding over judgment, you chip away at the walls built by shame and guilt, reinforcing your resilience and reclaiming your true self.

Healing the Inner Critic to Rebuild Self-Worth

One of the toughest obstacles in healing from childhood trauma is confronting the relentless voice of your inner critic. This inner critic is often the echo of cruel messages absorbed in early years—words spoken by caregivers, peers, or the environment that fed shame, doubt, and feelings of inadequacy. When trauma happens, this negative self-talk can become a default soundtrack, eroding even the strongest parts of your self-worth. Healing this voice isn't about silencing it instantly; it's about understanding where it comes from, why it lingers, and then gently but firmly changing the relationship you have with it.

The inner critic often masquerades as a form of 'protection'—a misguided attempt by your psyche to keep you safe from disappointment, failure, or rejection. It tries to warn you, to prevent you from making mistakes, even if it's harsh or cruel in its delivery. But here's the truth: this critic rarely protects. Instead, it traps you in a cycle of self-judgment that keeps the wounds of your childhood open and fresh. Recognizing this is the first step. Once you see the inner critic as a scared part of yourself rather than an objective judge, you gain the power to transform it.

Breaking free from this internal antagonist requires cultivating a voice that counters it with kindness and understanding. But that's easier said than done. You might find yourself questioning: how can I believe in myself when I'm so used to tearing myself down? The answer lies in consistency and patience. You won't silence or replace the inner critic overnight, but by gradually introducing compassion and truth, the grip of negativity loosens.

One effective approach is to identify the specific messages your inner critic delivers. What does it say when you try something new? When you're vulnerable? When you face setbacks? Once you've named these messages, you can challenge them. Ask yourself: "Is this true? Is there evidence to support this belief or is it just my trauma speaking?" Often, you'll find that these harsh feelings arise from distorted perspectives rooted in past pain, not present reality.

Another critical piece in this healing work is learning to speak to yourself with the empathy you wish you'd received as a child. Imagine the kind words your younger self needed but never heard. Practice affirming those words to yourself now. It can feel awkward initially, sometimes even unbelievable, but over time, these affirmations build a new neural pathway of self-respect and acceptance. When the inner critic speaks up, you'll be ready with a response—a compassionate truth that gently but firmly counters the old narrative of unworthiness.

Importantly, rebuilding your self-worth isn't just about internal dialogue; it's also about taking actions that reinforce your value. Setting boundaries, saying no when something doesn't align with your well-being, or pursuing activities that bring you joy and confidence all send clear messages to your inner critic: "I am worthy. I deserve respect." Every choice that honors you chips away at the critic's power and nurtures your authentic self.

Healing the inner critic is also a journey of reconnecting with that wounded inner child. This young part of yourself carries the raw feelings, fears, and unmet needs that fuel the critical voice today. By intentionally connecting with this inner child, often through journaling or visualization, you can begin to soothe those feelings and offer the love and safety that was missing. This compassionate connection often surprises people with how deeply it shifts their self-perception. It's not about fixing your inner child, because that part of you is not broken—it's about befriending and supporting the parts that have been hurt and silenced.

Therapists often describe this process as a form of reparenting. This means providing to yourself what others failed to provide—consistent care, validation, and acceptance. When you step into this role, the inner critic starts losing its grip because the child inside no longer feels abandoned or neglected. Instead, that child feels heard, safe, and loved. And from this foundation, your capacity to trust yourself and build genuine self-worth grows exponentially.

Another important nuance in addressing the inner critic is recognizing that it might not always sound negative. Sometimes, it wears the disguise of perfectionism, overachievement, or relentless productivity. These messages can seem empowering on the surface, pushing you to "do better" or "be stronger." But the underlying message often still shames and limits you, suggesting you're only valuable when you're meeting impossible standards. Healing involves spotting these disguised forms of criticism and gently reminding yourself that your worth is not conditional on performance or approval.

This healing work can feel emotionally intense and even scary at times. The critic may resist change with increased volume or hostility. It's here that patience and gentle persistence are essential. Developing a support system—whether through trusted friends, a therapist, or support groups—can provide the external validation and encouragement needed when the inner dialogue feels overwhelming. Remember, healing doesn't mean going it alone; it means learning to surround yourself with people and tools that affirm your inherent worth as you build that inner belief.

Rebuilding self-worth after trauma requires acknowledging that you are whole, just as you are, not because of what you do or how you appear to others, but simply because you exist. This truth may seem radical if you've spent years drowning in self-doubt, but holding onto it gently and consistently, even during moments when the critic shouts the loudest, is where real transformation begins.

It's also important to celebrate progress, no matter how small. Every time you catch the inner critic and offer a kinder response, you're rewiring your brain and reclaiming your power. Every boundary you establish or negative belief you challenge builds resilience. Over time, these moments accumulate, crafting a new self-narrative—one grounded in courage, compassion, and undeniable self-worth.

In the end, healing the inner critic is not just about silencing a voice; it's about reclaiming your right to be your full and authentic self. When you take these steps, the past loses its control, and a new self emerges—stronger, wiser, and worthy of love, beginning with the love you give yourself.

CHAPTER 3

RECLAIMING EMOTIONAL
FREEDOM

Stepping into emotional freedom means giving yourself permission to feel without judgment and to nurture the parts of you that were once silenced or wounded. It's about embracing self-compassion as a daily practice rather than a distant ideal, learning to listen to your inner voice with kindness instead of criticism. This chapter opens the door to reclaiming your power by gently reparenting yourself—offering the care and validation you might never have received—while equipping you with practical tools rooted in mindfulness, somatic awareness, and cognitive techniques that help calm the nervous system and reshape old patterns. It's a transformative process that invites rewriting the narrative you've lived by for so long, crafting a new story where you're not defined by pain but by resilience and hope. The road to reclaiming emotional freedom is rarely linear, but it's always possible, and every step forward is a testament to your courage and capacity to heal.

The Power of Self-Compassion and Cultivating Self-Love

Healing from childhood trauma is a profound and often difficult journey, but one of the most transformative forces within it is the ability to practice self-compassion and foster genuine self-love. These are not simply feel-good concepts; they are essential lifelines that can help you reclaim emotional freedom. When the wounds of your early years run deep, it becomes all too easy to carry a harsh inner critic—a voice that endlessly judges, shames, and dismisses your worth. Cultivating self-compassion allows you to counter that voice, replacing it with kindness and understanding.

To cultivate self-love after trauma means learning to accept yourself fully, even the parts you might have been taught to reject. You begin to see yourself not as a damaged or broken person, but as someone worthy of care and respect. This shift isn't about ignoring your pain or pretending everything is okay; instead, it's about acknowledging your struggles with a gentle heart and giving yourself permission to heal.

Trauma often leaves survivors stuck in patterns of self-blame or feeling unworthy of happiness. Those feelings aren't truths—they're painful echoes of the past that need to be gently challenged. Self-compassion is how you start rewriting that narrative by treating yourself as you would a beloved friend: offering patience, encouragement, and forgiveness where before there might have been only harsh judgment. This helps loosen the grip of shame and self-criticism, which are barriers to healing no matter how deeply entrenched they feel.

When you practice self-compassion, you create a secure internal environment where healing can begin. Think of it as creating a safe haven inside yourself, a place free of blame or unrealistic expectations. This inner sanctuary is crucial because it becomes the foundation for sustained emotional freedom. Without it, the process of healing can feel overwhelming, like swimming against a relentless current of negativity and doubt.

One common misconception about self-love is that it requires you to feel perfect or fully healed before accepting yourself. In reality, self-love thrives in the space of imperfection. It asks you to embrace your humanity, your vulnerabilities, and even your setbacks without losing respect for yourself. This acceptance isn't complacency; it's an active, courageous stance that says, "I'm worthy of care now, even as I work through my pain."

It's important to recognize that this is a process—cultivating self-compassion doesn't happen overnight. In the beginning, many people find it difficult to be kind to themselves, especially if the trauma resulted in years of internalized criticism. But with practice, each small act of self-kindness builds on the last, strengthening your ability to care for and protect your emotional well-being.

Self-love also opens the door to healthier relationships. Trauma often teaches us to doubt our value or fear intimacy. When you begin to truly value yourself, those patterns start to shift. You'll start attracting people who see and respect your worth and who support your healing rather than diminish it. In this way, self-compassion becomes a cornerstone not only of internal peace but also of external connection.

It's helpful to approach self-compassion with tangible actions as well as mindset shifts. This could mean setting aside quiet moments for yourself, speaking encouraging words aloud, practicing mindfulness techniques, or engaging in soothing activities that affirm your worth. These acts send a message to your brain that you are worthy of kindness. Over time, these repeated messages reshape your internal dialogue, softening the voice that once only criticized.

Another powerful way to nurture self-compassion is by acknowledging your resilience. Surviving trauma demands incredible strength, even if it doesn't always feel that way. When you honor your capacity to endure and keep going, you start to see your story not only through the lens of pain but also through the lens of courage and triumph. This perspective shifts the narrative from victimhood to empowerment.

Importantly, cultivating self-love doesn't mean isolating yourself from support. In fact, self-compassion includes recognizing when you need help and reaching out without judgment. It's about treating yourself as gently as possible while also being realistic and proactive in your healing journey. The balance of self-kindness and action creates momentum toward emotional freedom.

For many survivors, the practice of self-compassion can initially trigger discomfort or resistance because it challenges deeply ingrained beliefs about self-worth. It may awaken vulnerable emotions or unexpected grief. In these moments, it's crucial to hold space for whatever arises rather than push it away. Pain can coexist with compassion, and both are part of healing.

Self-love also empowers you to forgive—not necessarily to excuse the harm caused by others, but to release yourself from the heavy burden of resentment and bitterness. Forgiveness in this context is an act of liberation, freeing your heart and mind to embrace peace. It's a step toward reclaiming your emotional freedom from the grip of the past.

Developing self-compassion fuels emotional resilience, which is the ability to bounce back from difficulties without losing your sense of self-worth. This resilience becomes the armor you wear as you face triggers, setbacks, and hard memories. When your foundation is grounded in kindness toward yourself, you're less likely to be swept away by pain or discouragement.

The journey toward emotional freedom through self-compassion and self-love inevitably involves learning to listen deeply to yourself. This means tuning in to your needs, feelings, and limits without judgment. It means honoring your pace and recognizing that healing is highly personal and non-linear. Each step you take is an act of self-affirmation.

Finally, as you embrace these practices, it can be helpful to remind yourself that you aren't alone. Many who have endured childhood trauma have walked this path before you and found peace on the other side. The power of self-compassion lies in its ability to transform suffering into growth. It reclaims your narrative, restores your hope, and—above all—teaches you that you are worthy of love from the inside out, exactly as you are.

Reparenting Yourself: A Practical Guide to Self-Healing

Reparenting yourself is more than a therapeutic concept; it's a vital practice for healing the deep emotional wounds left by childhood trauma. When the caregivers who were supposed to nurture and protect you fell short—whether through neglect, inconsistency, or harm—the inner child that thrives within you carries those unmet needs and unresolved pain. Reparenting is the conscious act of giving yourself what you didn't receive early on: safety, understanding, validation, and unconditional love. It's a journey that asks you to step into the role of the compassionate parent your inner child longs for, shifting from survival mode to a conscious, nurturing presence.

At first, reparenting can feel strange or even intimidating. Our internal dialogue may resist this effort, sometimes echoing the critical voices we've internalized over years. That's natural. The path to healing is rarely straightforward, but the core of reparenting lies in developing a deep, ongoing relationship with yourself—especially the part that still feels vulnerable, scared, or overlooked. This relationship doesn't have to be perfect; it only needs to be honest and kind. Start by pausing to recognize what your inner child needs in any given moment. Maybe it's reassurance after a setback, or gentle encouragement when you're anxious. Learning to listen and respond with patience instead of judgment transforms the way you experience yourself.

A crucial step in reparenting is cultivating self-compassion. Unlike self-pity or indulgence, self-compassion involves treating your pain with a tenderness that supports growth. Imagine being your own advocate rather than your harshest critic. When the child inside berates you or blames you for past experiences, counter that narrative with understanding. This means acknowledging your difficulties and mistakes without shame, and recognizing that your reactions are rooted in survival rather than failure. Self-compassion builds emotional resilience because it rewires the brain's response to stress, shifting it away from fear and toward self-acceptance. This shift creates space for healing—space where your inner child feels safe enough to unfold their true self.

Reparenting also calls for setting clear, healthy boundaries, not because you want to isolate yourself but because you deserve to create an environment where you can thrive. When you think about how a nurturing parent protects their child from harm, you realize boundaries are acts of love and respect. They teach your inner child that it's okay to say no to people, situations, or beliefs that trigger feelings of unworthiness or danger. This might mean limiting contact with toxic influences, or simply allowing yourself to pause and step back when overwhelmed. Such boundaries are essential for emotional safety and for reclaiming your autonomy after years of feeling powerless.

The practical side of reparenting includes daily rituals that reinforce your inner child's sense of stability and care. Consistency is key here. Simple acts—like journaling your feelings, speaking kindly to yourself in moments of doubt, or engaging in calming activities—cultivate a sense of trust that perhaps didn't exist before. Think of these rituals as the bedtime stories, warm meals, or hugs that a caring parent might provide. Over time, these practices create a foundation of security that your nervous system craves, gradually replacing old patterns of self-neglect or self-criticism.

Many find that visualization exercises help anchor their reparenting efforts. You might picture your younger self experiencing the nurturing you missed— being held, reassured, or encouraged. Visualizations can also allow you to have an internal dialogue, where your present self listens to your inner child's fears and responds with empathy. This isn't about escaping reality; it's about rewriting the dialogue that shapes your emotional world. By doing so, you slowly transform not just your feelings, but the very lens through which you view yourself and the world around you.

It's important to recognize that reparenting is not a one-time fix but an ongoing conversation with yourself. Healing childhood trauma means unraveling years of ingrained beliefs and reactions, which don't disappear overnight. Patience becomes your ally here, as does gentle perseverance. On some days, the inner critic may roar louder, and the wounds might feel fresh. Those moments don't mean you're off track. Instead, they're reminders of where healing work is still needed. Treat those instances as a call to double down on your nurturing practices, to reassure your inner child that they are safe and that you are there for them now.

Another powerful element of reparenting is learning to recognize and celebrate your strengths and achievements from a place of authentic self-love. Childhood trauma often eclipses feelings of competence and worth, but part of healing is reclaiming your sense of identity free from past limitations. When you acknowledge your resilience—the fact that you survived and kept going—you honor the courage your inner child displayed every day. Celebrate small victories, whether it's setting a boundary, acknowledging a painful emotion without judgment, or simply making it through a difficult moment. These celebrations are like the encouraging words a good parent offers, reinforcing that you matter and you're capable.

It's also essential to create a safe external environment that mirrors your internal efforts. Surround yourself with people who respect your boundaries and uplift your journey toward healing. If your support system doesn't feel safe or nurturing, consider reaching out to professionals or support groups familiar with childhood trauma recovery. These resources can provide important validation and guidance as you learn to parent yourself. Remember, reparenting isn't about isolation; it's about forming relationships rooted in respect—with yourself and others.

As you deepen your reparenting practice, you may notice shifts in how you respond emotionally and behaviorally. Triggers might lose their intensity, and the overwhelming waves of shame or fear may soften. Your nervous system will gradually learn that it doesn't have to remain in a constant state of alert or freeze. That's a profound change, one that moves you toward genuine emotional freedom—the heart of this chapter's mission. With each act of self-nurturing, you're not just healing old wounds; you're rewriting the story of your life. The child you once were begins to feel seen, heard, and loved, which opens the door for you to fully embrace the adult you've become.

Learning to reparent yourself is, at its core, about reclaiming control of your emotional world. It's about taking responsibility not for the trauma inflicted on you but for your healing journey going forward. This process demands courage because it asks you to face your pain with openness rather than avoidance. Yet, it also offers one of the most profound gifts: the ability to build a relationship with yourself that is compassionate, empowering, and unwavering. In that relationship lies the freedom to feel whole again—and to live a life no longer haunted by the shadows of the past.

Remember, every act of reparenting, no matter how small, is a declaration that you deserve kindness and care. When you extend that kindness inward, you set the foundation for all other healing work to flourish. Reparenting yourself isn't just about fixing what was broken; it's about nurturing the infinite potential of the person you are becoming. As you continue this journey, may you find strength in your vulnerability and peace in knowing that the love you offer yourself is the truest form of emotional freedom.

Coping Tools That Actually Work: Somatic Techniques, CBT, Mindfulness, and More

When you've been carrying the weight of childhood trauma, finding ways to cope that actually help—not just distract—can feel overwhelming. There's a vast world of self-help advice out there, some of it helpful, some less so. But the truth is, healing demands tools that are both accessible and effective, tools that engage your mind and body in a way that brings real change. This section focuses on some of the most proven approaches to gaining emotional freedom: somatic techniques, cognitive-behavioral therapy (CBT), mindfulness, and more. These aren't just buzzwords;

they're lifelines that countless survivors have used to reclaim their inner peace and build resilience.

Somatic techniques stand out because they connect you back to your body—a place often neglected or even feared after trauma. When trauma lodges itself in your nervous system, your body remembers what your mind wants to forget. Somatic work helps you notice these physical sensations without judgment, teaching you to regulate your body's response to stress. Simple practices like deep breathing, grounding exercises, or gentle movement can soften the body's defensive armor and release tension you've been holding unconsciously. Over time, this reconnection empowers you to feel safer in your own skin, reducing symptoms like anxiety and panic that often worsen when your body is stuck on high alert.

CBT, or cognitive-behavioral therapy, provides another vital method of coping that can dramatically reshape how you interpret and respond to your thoughts and feelings. Childhood trauma often installs a harsh inner critic and unhelpful thinking patterns—"I'm not enough," "I'm unlovable," or "I have to be perfect to be safe." CBT works by helping you become aware of these automatic thoughts, challenge their validity, and replace them with healthier, more balanced beliefs. It's a practical, step-by-step approach that equips you with mental tools to turn the volume down on shame, guilt, and fear. While it takes commitment, many find CBT principles can be learned and practiced both inside and outside of therapy, making it a powerful self-empowering strategy.

Mindfulness, though often described in spiritual or mystical terms, is deceptively simple and profoundly effective. At its core, mindfulness means paying attention—on purpose, nonjudgmentally, and moment by moment. For survivors of childhood trauma, this kind of awareness can create space between you and your triggers, reactions, or overwhelming emotions. Instead of being swept away by flashbacks, shame, or anger, mindfulness encourages you to observe these experiences with curiosity and compassion. The consistent practice of mindfulness has been shown to reduce symptoms of PTSD, depression, and anxiety by rewiring how your brain processes stress. It invites you to live more fully in the present, reclaiming control over where you place your attention.

Integrating these methods doesn't mean you have to master them all immediately or follow a rigid routine. Healing is nonlinear and deeply personal. Some days, you might gravitate toward somatic exercises that soothe your nervous system. Other times, journaling about your thoughts or practicing CBT techniques may be more accessible. The key is to explore what feels right and sustainable for your unique journey. The process of practicing these tools itself fosters a sense of agency—you're no longer at the mercy of past wounds but actively rewriting your responses and reclaiming your power.

Beyond these core techniques, there are several other coping tools that complement and enhance your emotional freedom. Expressive arts like writing, drawing, or music offer ways to release feelings that words alone can't capture. Movement-based therapies such as yoga or dance help integrate body and mind, transforming stuck energy into a source of vitality. Developing a ritual of self-care, no matter how small or simple, can gradually rebuild your relationship with yourself as someone worthy of kindness and attention. These practices remind you that healing is multidimensional—it involves nurturing your physical, emotional, and spiritual self.

It's also important to recognize that coping tools serve as bridges, not destinations. They prepare and support you to face deeper layers of trauma when you're ready. At first, their function might be to help you feel grounded and stable. Over time, they become part of a larger framework of self-awareness and growth. This evolution often shifts your relationship with trauma— from feeling overwhelmed by it to understanding and owning your story without shame. By regularly engaging in these practices, you foster resilience and cultivate an inner sanctuary where healing can continue to unfold.

The power of these tools lies not only in their techniques but in the kindness and patience you bring to their use. Everyone's nervous system, history, and rhythm of healing are different. If you find a method frustrating or exhausting at first, that's okay. The invitation is simply to keep showing up, however imperfectly. Each small step is a radical act of love toward yourself. This consistency lays a foundation for reclaiming your emotional freedom—the freedom to experience your feelings fully, to calm your nervous system, and to rewrite the story of your inner life.

For mental health professionals and loved ones supporting survivors, understanding these tools is equally vital. They represent pathways to help people feel heard, safe, and empowered. Encouraging a trauma survivor to try somatic practices or CBT exercises can open doors to progress when verbal talk therapy alone feels too daunting. Modeling mindfulness or self-compassion cultivates an environment where healing is nurtured with patience and respect. As much as these tools serve the individual, they also strengthen the web of support around them, creating a relational container that honors the complexity of trauma recovery.

Ultimately, coping tools that actually work are those that honor the whole person—you, with your body, brain, and heart intertwined. They invite you to meet yourself with courage and tenderness, to break free from habitual survival patterns, and to step into a life where emotional freedom is not just possible, but your lived reality. This isn't about perfection or erasing the past. It's about carving out spaces within yourself where healing can flourish and where your future is no longer chained by childhood pain.

Rewriting Your Story to Create a New Empowered Identity

Our stories shape how we see ourselves and the world around us. But what happens when the story we've been told, or have told ourselves, is rooted in pain from childhood trauma? Often, these narratives paint us as victims, flawed, or unworthy, trapping us in cycles of limitation and self-doubt. Reclaiming your emotional freedom involves more than just understanding your past—it calls for an intentional rewriting of your internal story, crafting an identity built on strength, resilience, and hope.

This process isn't about denying the hardships or dismissing what you endured. Instead, it's about honoring your experiences without allowing them to define your present or dictate your future. Think of your story as a book with many chapters—just because some chapters were painful or unfair doesn't mean the entire story is bleak. You get to be the author deciding how the next chapters unfold, creating a narrative where you are not just surviving but thriving.

Rewriting your story begins by recognizing the unconscious scripts that have guided your beliefs about yourself. These scripts often come from early experiences and might say things like "I am not good enough," "I must always please others," or "I am unlovable." These messages, though ingrained, aren't inherently true—they're simply echoes of survival mechanisms formed in response to trauma. The first step toward transformation is to gently uncover and challenge these limiting beliefs.

As you become aware of these inner narratives, you can begin questioning their accuracy. Where did this belief come from? Does it truly reflect who you are or just who you were forced to be under certain circumstances? What evidence exists that contradicts these negative beliefs? This kind of inquiry helps weaken their hold on you, making room for new, empowering perspectives to take root.

One of the most powerful tools in rewriting your story is reframing. This means looking at painful experiences with fresh eyes—acknowledging the difficulties but also recognizing your courage, resourcefulness, and the strength it took to survive. For example, what once felt like weakness or failure can transform into a testament of resilience and tenacity. Your survival itself is proof of your inner power, a fact that deserves celebration, not shame.

Building a new identity also calls for embracing your whole self, including traits and qualities that trauma might have obscured. Perhaps your creativity, your kindness, or your intelligence were overshadowed by feelings of unworthiness. Reclaiming your story means shining light on these authentic parts of you, nurturing them, and allowing them to grow. This can be a slow process, often requiring patience and self-compassion, but it's fundamental to creating a self-image rooted in truth rather than trauma.

It's important to remember that rewriting your story doesn't mean erasing your history or pretending everything is okay. Instead, it means recognizing that your past is just one element of who you are—not the entirety. You're learning to hold both your pain and your strengths at the same time, weaving them together into a narrative that reflects survival, growth, and possibility.

This new narrative affects more than just how you see yourself internally—it transforms how you engage with the world. When your story shifts from one of victimhood to empowerment, your choices, relationships, and goals also change. You become less bound by old patterns and more open to opportunities that affirm your worth. You start setting boundaries not out of fear or guilt, but out of self-respect and clarity about your needs.

Crafting this empowered identity is not a one-time event. It's an ongoing journey that involves revisiting your story whenever old wounds resurface or new challenges arise. Each time you reclaim your narrative, you reinforce your sense of self, making it stronger and more resilient. With practice, this internal rewriting becomes more natural, allowing you to live with greater authenticity and emotional freedom.

Another aspect of creating a new story involves envisioning the future you want rather than the one your trauma predicted. Envision who you want to become, what values you'll stand for, and the kind of life that feels fulfilling. This imaginative work helps reorient your energy toward growth and healing, providing you a compass to navigate life beyond the shadows of trauma. Your story becomes not just about where you came from, but where you're headed.

Surrounding yourself with supportive people who honor this new version of you is vital too. When friends, family, or professionals acknowledge and reinforce your empowered identity, it helps solidify the changes you're making inside. Their validation provides an external mirror reflecting the truth of your growth, which can be especially important when old stories threaten to pull you back into familiar pain.

Writing exercises, journaling, or storytelling can be practical ways to practice rewriting your story. Putting words to your experience allows you to organize and process feelings, noticing patterns or gaps you might not have seen before. It also offers a safe space to experiment with new ways of framing your journey—highlighting moments of strength, kindness, and courage that have always existed but may have been buried under trauma.

Sometimes, rewriting your story means naming and rejecting the lies you were told. It means learning to speak kindly to yourself instead of harshly, reclaiming your voice after years of silence or self-censorship. It also means claiming your identity beyond trauma labels—reminding yourself that while trauma is part of your experience, it is not your entire identity.

The process is deeply personal and unique to each individual, so it's essential to move at your own pace. It's okay to take breaks, revisit previous chapters of healing, and gather strength before pushing further. The goal isn't to rush but to build a sustainable foundation for well-being that honors where you've been and where you want to go.

In the end, rewriting your story is an act of courage. It's choosing to believe in yourself when doubt has been the louder voice for too long. You're redefining what "possible" looks like for you and stepping into a future where your past does not have to limit your happiness or sense of worth.

By embracing this process, you reclaim emotional freedom—not because the past disappears, but because you no longer need to be defined or controlled by it. You become the author of your own narrative, with the pen firmly in your hand, ready to write a story infused with strength, healing, and hope.

CHAPTER 4

MOVING FORWARD WITH
STRENGTH

Healing from childhood trauma isn't about erasing the past but learning to walk forward with resilience and courage, even when the scars remain. It means embracing the messy, imperfect journey of rebuilding trust—not just with others but with yourself—and recognizing that strength doesn't always roar; sometimes it's the quiet decision to keep going when giving up feels easier. This chapter invites you to honor the progress you've made while preparing you to face challenges with renewed hope and grounded confidence, understanding that growth is ongoing and healing isn't linear. By cultivating patience and self-compassion, you can hold space for setbacks without losing sight of the freedom and peace you're working toward, knowing that reaching out for support isn't a sign of weakness but an act of bravery and self-respect.

Building Healthy Relationships After Childhood Trauma

One of the most challenging yet transformative steps in healing from childhood trauma involves learning to build healthy relationships. Trauma often distorts our understanding of trust, safety, and connection, making intimacy feel risky or impossible. When your earliest bonds were marked by neglect, abuse, or unpredictability, it's no surprise if you find yourself struggling to connect authentically with others in adulthood. However, it is absolutely possible to create relationships that nurture, support, and empower you rather than drain or harm you.

Healing from childhood trauma means relearning relationship dynamics from the ground up. This process isn't about rushing to form connections or forcing trust; instead, it's about approaching relationships with gentleness and self-awareness. You first need to cultivate a clear sense of your own needs, limits, and values. Without this inner clarity, it becomes difficult to communicate effectively or recognize when a relationship is unsafe or unhealthy. This self-knowledge acts as an internal compass, helping you navigate your interactions with more confidence and less anxiety.

For survivors of childhood trauma, emotional vulnerability can often feel like a double-edged sword. On one hand, showing vulnerability is necessary for real connection; on the other, it may trigger fears of rejection or abuse. Practicing vulnerability requires courage and a strong foundation of self-trust that you're actively building through therapy, reflection, or supportive communities. You have to become comfortable showing up as your authentic self—even when it feels scary—which means being honest about your experiences, your fears, and your hopes without feeling ashamed or minimized.

It's normal to wrestle with fear when opening up to others. You might ask yourself, "Can I really trust this person?" or "What if I get hurt again?" Instead of letting these worries paralyze you, use them as important signals. They tell you when to slow down or when to pay attention to red flags. Healthy relationships don't develop overnight; they evolve through a series of small, consistent acts of trust and respect. Being mindful and intentional can help you differentiate between someone who respects your boundaries and someone who doesn't.

Boundaries emerge as a cornerstone for building those healthier connections. Setting boundaries for yourself and expecting others to respect them is a revolutionary act when you consider how often trauma involves boundary violations. Healthy boundaries aren't walls to keep people out but rather clear guidelines that protect your emotional and physical well-being. They are the lines you draw around how you want to be treated, and maintaining them is a lifelong practice that helps prevent the old patterns of being overwhelmed or exploited.

One of the most empowering aspects of building new relationships after trauma is discovering that you can choose whom to keep close—and whom to keep at a distance. This choice itself can feel radical when your earlier life circumstances may have felt trapped or dictated by others. You get to decide whom to invite in, how much to share, and what kind of support feels nourishing to you. Over time, these choices reinforce a newfound sense of agency and safety in your relationships.

Healing also means becoming attuned to the difference between codependency and healthy interdependence. Childhood trauma can blur these lines, causing someone to either overextend themselves emotionally to "fix" others or avoid any closeness altogether. In contrast, healthy relationships thrive on mutual respect, balanced give-and-take, and a shared commitment to individual growth. Both partners can maintain their sense of self while being fully present for each other. Learning to ask for what you need and receive support without guilt or fear is a key milestone in this transition.

Another challenge to anticipate is the possibility of encountering relationships that mirror aspects of your traumatic past. It's not unusual to unconsciously gravitate toward familiar dysfunction because the patterns feel strangely comfortable, even if painful. Recognizing these repeating patterns can be painful but also liberating. Once you see them clearly, you can consciously decide to step out of old cycles and seek healthier connections instead. Sometimes this means letting go of people who don't honor your healing process, which can be an act of tremendous self-care even if it feels difficult or lonely at first.

Genuine connection requires patience—both with yourself and others. It's important to understand that healing relationships aren't about perfection or never making mistakes. Rather, they revolve around compassion, forgiveness, and the willingness to grow together. You might find that some relationships weather storms and come out stronger, while others simply aren't meant to continue. That's okay. Each relationship is an opportunity to practice your boundaries, your vulnerability, and your worthiness.

Communicating openly and assertively is an essential skill to nurture as you build healthier relationships. This isn't always easy, especially if trauma taught you to prioritize others' needs over your own or to expect conflict from sharing your truth. Practice being clear and calm about what you want and need without falling into blame or defensiveness. Assertiveness means your voice is valued—it does not mean you have to fight or prove yourself. Over time, this honest communication helps to create environments where everyone feels safe and respected.

It's also vital to find or nurture spaces where you feel seen and understood—not judged or dismissed. This might be through friendships, intimate partnerships, support groups, or communities where emotional safety is prioritized. When you surround yourself with people who get it, who honor your experiences, and who encourage your growth, it reinforces your healing journey. Being witnessed with empathy and respect is profoundly validating and can rebuild the fractured parts of self-esteem that trauma often shatters.

Remember, as you cultivate healthier relationships, the relationship you have with yourself remains the foundation. You must continue investing in your self-compassion and self-trust. When you show up for yourself consistently—listening to your feelings, meeting your needs, forgiving your mistakes—you train your brain and heart to expect kindness and dignity in relationships. This internal work makes it easier to attract and sustain relationships that mirror the respect you're learning to grant yourself.

Taking these steps doesn't mean your past trauma disappears, nor does it erase the pain you've experienced. Instead, it creates space where you can live and love more freely, where trauma doesn't dictate your worth or your ability to connect. You're building a new way forward—one relationship at a time—that honors your resilience and celebrates your capacity to heal. With each healthy connection, you reinforce the truth that trauma, while impactful, doesn't have to be the defining story of your life.

Building healthy relationships after childhood trauma is a journey of reclaiming your voice, your boundaries, and your capacity to trust. It takes courage, patience, and a willingness to confront uncomfortable feelings, but the rewards are profound. Through this process, you discover that you are not broken, but whole and deserving of love on your terms. As you move forward with strength, you are also stepping into a future where connection is a source of healing rather than harm—an essential part of living a life that truly feels like your own.

Maintaining Your Healing Progress Over Time

Healing from childhood trauma isn't a one-time event—it's an ongoing process that requires gentle persistence and active care. The progress you've made is precious, and maintaining it means cultivating habits and mindsets that support your growth every day. This doesn't mean perfection or never feeling setbacks. Instead, it's about recognizing healing as a lifelong commitment, one that respects your human complexity and the ebb and flow of emotional life.

One of the most important things in sustaining your healing journey is developing a deeper connection with yourself. After years of surviving patterns and coping mechanisms, it can be easy to slip back into old ways without even realizing it. That's why becoming mindful of your thoughts and emotions is crucial. By tuning in regularly—through journaling, meditation, or quiet reflection—you create a safe space where you can observe your inner world without judgment or rushing to fix things. This practice anchors you in self-awareness, which is the foundation for preventing old wounds from reactivating unchecked.

It is also vital to honor the limits of your energy and emotional capacity. Recovering from trauma often means learning how to pace yourself differently. You might find that some days feel incredibly strong and resilient, while other days bring fatigue, frustration, or despair. Both are part of the process. Understanding that these fluctuations are natural helps you avoid harsh self-criticism when life doesn't go according to plan. Instead, you can respond with compassion, adjusting your expectations and care strategies as needed. Over time, this practice creates emotional flexibility, which is a key component in long-term healing.

Staying connected to a community of support can't be overstated. Whether it's trusted friends, family, a therapist, or a support group, having people who understand your journey makes maintaining progress simpler and less lonely. They can remind you of your strengths when you forget them and hold space for you when you feel vulnerable. This network acts like a safety net during moments of uncertainty, enabling you to take risks in your healing without losing your footing. Keep in mind that choosing who to trust is part of your healing—surround yourself with individuals who honor your boundaries and uplift your growth.

Rituals and routines that nurture your well-being are another pillar for maintaining healing. These don't have to be elaborate or time-consuming—small, consistent actions like drinking water mindfully, taking short walks in nature, or engaging in creative outlets can provide grounding and joy. Such rituals create a rhythm that supports your mental and emotional health, making healing an integrated part of daily life instead of a separate task to accomplish. When life's chaos intensifies, these routines act as touchstones that bring you back to your center.

Part of sustaining your progress involves continuing to challenge and expand your understanding of yourself. Healing opens up new possibilities for who you can be, but that process requires curiosity and courage. You might discover parts of yourself you never knew existed or uncover emotions that were buried beneath layers of survival. Facing these truths isn't easy, but it's necessary for growth. Inviting honesty into your life—including accepting your imperfections and vulnerabilities—allows for a more authentic experience of peace and resilience.

It's also critical to remember that healing isn't linear. There will be moments when old triggers catch you off guard or you feel stuck in familiar negative patterns. When this happens, patience is key. Instead of seeing these moments as failures, view them as invitations to dig deeper into your healing work. Reflect on what these experiences reveal about your needs or boundaries that may need reevaluation. Being gentle with yourself during setbacks teaches you resilience— the ability to bounce back and keep moving forward despite difficulty.

Another essential aspect of maintaining your healing progress lies in celebrating your wins—both big and small. Too often, trauma survivors underplay their achievements because they're overshadowed by the weight of past pain. But recognizing your growth, no matter how incremental, fuels motivation and self-confidence. It reaffirms that change is happening and that you're capable of leading a more fulfilling life. Whether it's setting a boundary, expressing your needs clearly, or simply being kinder to yourself on a tough day, acknowledge these moments as victories on your path.

Maintaining progress also involves being intentional about what you allow into your life—this includes people, environments, habits, and information. Trauma can sometimes distort your sense of safety, so it's important to curate your surroundings mindfully. This might mean distancing yourself from toxic relationships or limiting exposure to media that heightens anxiety or shame. Protecting your emotional space gives you the clarity and peace to continue healing. It's a way of honoring the work you've done and valuing your well-being.

As your healing goes deeper, you might also find that your definition of self-care evolves. It moves beyond bubble baths and occasional treats into a more robust framework that supports your emotional, psychological, and physical health consistently. This might include learning how to advocate for yourself in healthcare, developing skills for managing stress, or even pursuing passions that enrich your sense of purpose. When self-care becomes an integral part of who you are, it supports not just survival, but thriving.

Finally, staying open to professional guidance over time helps maintain the progress you've made. Healing from childhood trauma can bring up complex feelings, meaning it's valuable to have skilled professionals who can provide insight and tools when needed. Regular check-ins with therapists, counselors, or coaches ensure that you don't carry heavy burdens alone and that your healing continues to grow in healthy ways. Remember, reaching out for help is a sign of strength— not weakness—and part of honoring your ongoing journey.

In summary, maintaining your healing progress over time is about embracing a compassionate, flexible, and proactive approach to your mental and emotional health. It's about nurturing your inner connection, pacing yourself wisely, surrounding yourself with supportive relationships, and integrating healing into your everyday routines. By honoring the realities of ups and downs and celebrating your resilience, you build a foundation for lasting change. This ongoing commitment isn't just about moving forward—it's about moving forward with strength, grounded in self-love and the profound knowledge that your healing journey is one of empowerment and hope.

Knowing When to Seek Help: Therapy, Support Groups, and Coaching

Healing from childhood trauma is a courageous journey, but it's one that no one has to walk alone. Even with the most determined efforts toward self-healing, everyone reaches moments when personal resources aren't enough. These are the times when seeking outside support can become a powerful catalyst for change. Knowing when to reach out for therapy, join support groups, or seek coaching is key to moving forward with strength and gaining the clarity and resilience necessary to build a vibrant, healthy life.

Therapy often represents the first step many take on this path. A skilled therapist acts as a compassionate witness, someone trained to help you gently untangle the complex emotions, memories, and patterns rooted in your childhood wounds. It's not about "fixing" you, because you're not broken, but about providing a safe space to explore your truth without judgment. Sometimes, trauma can feel so overwhelming or confusing that it's impossible to face it alone. Therapy encourages a deeper understanding of the impact trauma has had on your body and mind, breaking down the walls you may have built to survive—walls that can later become barriers to connection, joy, and peace.

Yet, therapy isn't a one-size-fits-all solution, and that's okay. Different approaches resonate uniquely with each person. Some find solace in long-term talk therapy, others prefer expressive arts, somatic therapy, or trauma-focused cognitive behavioral therapy. What matters most is learning to recognize when you need that structured support and having the courage to ask for it. This moment of acknowledgment is itself an act of strength and self-love.

Support groups offer a different kind of healing atmosphere—one rooted in shared experience. There's immense power in gathering with others who truly understand the weight of childhood trauma because they've carried it too. The sense of isolation that so often accompanies trauma can begin to lift in these groups. You're not just heard; you're seen and validated. Hearing others' stories and offering your own can help break through layers of shame and silence, fostering a sense of belonging that so many survivors desperately need.

Being part of a support group doesn't mean you rely solely on the group to heal. Instead, it complements individual efforts and therapy, creating a broader safety net. It's a place where you can test out new ways of communicating, practice vulnerability, and witness resilience in the people around you. Sometimes, the simple act of knowing you're not alone sparks hope and motivation to keep going.

Coaching, on the other hand, often appeals to those who have made initial strides in understanding their trauma and want more focused guidance on moving forward. Unlike therapy, which may spend a lot of time on understanding and processing past pain, coaching tends to be more future-oriented and goal-driven. It's about creating actionable plans to build the life you envision—improving relationships, strengthening emotional regulation, or developing new habits that reinforce your well-being.

Choosing coaching doesn't mean you've "graduated" from therapy; many people benefit from integrating both. A trauma-informed coach acts as a supportive partner who encourages accountability, growth, and confidence, helping keep you grounded as you navigate challenges and celebrate victories. This kind of support can be particularly helpful when you feel stuck or overwhelmed by the practicalities of daily living after trauma.

Of course, no one wants to feel like they've "failed" by needing help. On the contrary, seeking assistance is a sign of incredible wisdom and bravery. Trauma, especially from childhood, doesn't usually fade simply by willing it away or "toughing it out." It requires intentional care, patience, and sometimes the guidance of trained professionals or the strength of collective support. If you find yourself repeatedly overwhelmed, struggling to maintain progress, or feeling isolated despite your efforts, it's a clear indication that outside help can be a lifeline rather than a last resort.

Sometimes people hesitate to ask for help because of the stigma around mental health or a belief that they have to manage their pain alone. This cultural myth needs dismantling. Trauma lives in isolation, but healing thrives in connection. By embracing support, you open a door to new perspectives and healthier ways to cope. You give yourself permission to be human—imperfect, wounded, yet deeply capable of growth and transformation.

There's also a practical aspect to consider. Trauma can create physiological changes in the brain and body that make emotional regulation and decision-making more difficult. A mental health professional can help retrain these systems through evidence-based methods that you likely won't be able to do on your own. Support groups provide that social nourishment which many survivors missed as children, helping repair the ability to trust and feel safe with others. Coaching encourages breaking down overwhelming goals into manageable steps, which can prevent discouragement and increase momentum.

Ultimately, your healing won't look like anyone else's. You will find a unique combination of supports that fits your needs and your personality. Some people might benefit from intense clinical therapy, while others find group settings or coaching sessions more empowering. Many discover that a blend of all three helps them create a balanced network of care. What matters is honoring your own rhythm and recognizing the moments when additional guidance can elevate your journey forward.

The decision to seek help often grows out of a deep inner knowing—a soft whisper amid the noise of everyday life that says, "I need support to keep moving." It might come from exhaustion with repeating negative patterns, a sense of reaching a plateau in healing, or a sudden realization that you deserve more than mere survival. Whatever form it takes, listening to that voice is a revolutionary act of self-respect.

Remember too, that asking for help doesn't commit you to any particular path forever. Therapy, groups, and coaching are tools you can explore and adjust as your needs evolve. They are flexible resources rather than fixed destinations. And alongside these resources, cultivating self-compassion and patience will sustain your progress, reminding you that healing is a dynamic process, not a checklist to complete.

In moments of vulnerability, reaching out for assistance is an act of strength that propels you toward freedom from the pain of childhood trauma. It reconnects you with your innate resilience and unlocks the potential for a life lived with greater peace, connection, and joy. You are not alone in this, and the right kind of help can amplify the power you already carry inside.

Embracing Peace: Living a Life You No Longer Need to Escape From

There comes a moment in the healing journey when the world no longer feels like a place you have to run away from. After years of wrestling with the shadows of childhood trauma, learning to embrace peace means stepping into a life where you aren't burdened by the need to escape. This peace isn't about perfection or erasing pain—it's about living fully, even with scars, and finding steadiness amidst the chaos that once defined your existence. It's the profound shift where survival mode dissolves and you start living from a place of strength, acceptance, and hope.

For so many adults who carry childhood wounds, escape was once the default mode. Whether it was through numbing, people-pleasing, avoidance, or dissociation, these strategies provided momentary relief from overwhelming truths you couldn't face as a child and sometimes still can't fully confront as an adult. But as you cultivate peace, you're learning that you don't have to flee anymore. You're safe now, not just physically but emotionally. The real work becomes about remaining present with your feelings, honoring your experience, and embracing life's imperfections without the impulse to run.

Living free from the need to escape requires a radical kind of courage—and patience. Sometimes peace comes quietly, like a gentle tide rolling in, and other times it arrives after a storm of self-reflection and uncovering raw emotions you thought were long buried. In these moments, peace doesn't feel comfortable. It feels unfamiliar and, at times, unsettling. But peace also creates space for something invaluable: authenticity. When you aren't hiding behind defenses or distractions, you begin to live in alignment with your true self, your values, and your deepest desires.

One truth emerges clearly on this journey: peace isn't a destination, it's a way of living. It means waking up without the crushing weight of old fears pressing down on your chest every morning. It means being able to fully experience joy without guilt or an unsettling feeling that it won't last. It means accepting yourself— flaws, triggers, and all—as a whole and worthy person. And in doing so, you break the cycle of trauma that once tried to define your life.

How do you go about embracing this kind of peace? It starts with reclaiming your sense of safety, which goes far beyond locking doors or creating physical boundaries. It's about creating internal safety, a sanctuary inside your mind and body where you feel supported and cared for. This internal refuge might take the form of mindfulness practices, soothing self-talk, or sensory rituals that ground you when anxiety rises. When you build trust with yourself and your environment in this way, those old patterns of escape lose their grip.

Another vital piece is forgiveness—not necessarily forgiving the source of trauma right away— but forgiving yourself for things you've done in response to pain. Maybe you escaped through addiction or pushed people away. Maybe you felt like you failed to protect yourself. Holding onto self-judgment just keeps the cycle spinning. Forgiveness offers a release valve; it opens the door to self-compassion, which softens the harshness many survivors carry inside. This doesn't mean ignoring accountability, but recognizing that survival was once your only option and you did the best you could with what you had.

Living without escape also means embracing vulnerability. This can feel paradoxical if your early years taught you to hide your feelings as a matter of survival. Yet, vulnerability is the doorway to genuine connection and belonging. When you allow yourself to be seen—even your messy, broken parts—you create opportunities for authentic relationships to flourish. Building these healthy connections reinforces your sense of belonging and safety in a way that trauma once stole from you.

Peace, then, is not a passive state; it requires active participation. It's a practice of showing up for yourself, even on the days when your trauma makes it hard to believe in healing. You keep choosing growth over comfort, awareness over avoidance. And with each choice, you weaken the compulsive need to escape and strengthen your capacity to live fully here and now.

One of the greatest gifts of embracing peace is reclaiming your time and energy. Trauma often hijacks your focus, redirecting your resources to managing triggers or emotional wounds. When peace begins to take root, you find yourself more present in ordinary moments—a morning coffee with gratitude, a walk outside feeling the sunlight, a conversation where you listen without fear. These moments become evidence that a life without constant escape is possible, and they offer proof that joy and calm can coexist alongside past pain.

It's also important to note that embracing peace means accepting that setbacks will occur. Healing isn't linear. There will be days when old wounds flare up and the urge to retreat is strong. This doesn't mean failure; it means you're human and that healing is a lifelong process. Being at peace includes extending kindness to yourself in these moments. You don't have to jump back into escape or shame—you can pause, breathe, and remind yourself that peace is built over time, brick by brick.

For those supporting trauma survivors, understanding what embracing peace looks like is just as crucial. It means offering space for autonomy and trusting that your loved one can find their way at their own pace. It means recognizing that peace isn't a quick fix or a neat resolution but an ongoing commitment to healing and presence. Encouragement, patience, and consistent support become cornerstones in this delicate process.

Ultimately, embracing peace means weaving your past, present, and future into a narrative that empowers rather than confines. Your trauma no longer defines your identity but becomes part of a complex, resilient story that includes hope, courage, and love. Living without the need to escape is both a triumph and an open invitation—to engage deeply with life, embrace its uncertainties, and discover that peace was inside you all along.

YOUR PATH TO LASTING EMOTIONAL FREEDOM

Healing from childhood trauma is not a simple destination but a lifelong journey, and as you reach this point in your path, it's important to honor the distance you've traveled. Every step you've taken—from recognizing old wounds to embracing new ways of being—reflects your courage and commitment to reclaim your life on your own terms. Emotional freedom isn't about erasing the past, but learning how to live fully in spite of it, growing stronger through every challenge you face.

What's powerful about this journey is that it invites you to rewrite your narrative in a way that's authentic and self-compassionate. You've likely done the hard work of understanding how trauma shaped your inner world, and now it's time to trust that you can continue to dismantle the old stories that no longer serve you. This is a process of both unlearning harmful patterns and intentionally cultivating new beliefs that nurture resilience, peace, and self-worth.

It's worth acknowledging the weight of this transformation. Breaking free from childhood trauma means reshaping how you relate to yourself and others, confronting painful emotions, and sometimes stepping into the unknown. The act of moving forward takes bravery because it challenges the survival strategies you leaned on in the past, yet no longer fit who you want to be. Holding that tension—the pull between old safety nets and new horizons—is part of what makes emotional freedom so profound and lasting.

One of the deepest truths in healing is that emotional freedom requires ongoing presence with yourself. This means tuning into what your body, heart, and mind need at any given moment and responding with kindness rather than judgment. The pace of your healing may vary, and there might be days that feel easy and others where progress feels a little harder. Both are a natural part of the terrain. Rather than becoming frustrated when setbacks occur, cultivate curiosity about what these moments are teaching you. Often, they reveal areas still needing attention or moments to reinforce self-care.

Importantly, lasting emotional freedom means embracing your inherent worthiness. You've learned how trauma tried to convince you otherwise—that you were broken, unlovable, or not enough. But now you have the chance to see yourself through kinder eyes, the eyes of someone who acknowledges both your pain and your potential. This shift is not just empowering but essential. It lays the foundation for healthier relationships, authentic connections, and a sense of safety within yourself that can't be shaken by external circumstances.

Support continues to play a crucial role on this path. While your work begins within, building a community around you—whether through trusted friends, loved ones, or mental health professionals—helps hold you when the journey gets difficult. No one has to walk this road alone. And knowing when to ask for help is a sign of strength, not weakness. It's a reminder that healing is rarely linear and that reaching out expands your capacity to grow, adapt, and thrive.

As you move forward, remember that emotional freedom is not about perfection or the absence of pain; it's about living in alignment with your truth, even when life presents new challenges. It's about cultivating resilience so that when triggers arise, you respond with awareness rather than automatic reactions. The tools and insights you have gathered along the way empower you to shift from surviving to truly living. That transformation, no matter how gradual, is a testament to your inner strength.

There's also beauty in reclaiming your voice after trauma. Childhood experiences might have silenced you or made you question your worth. Now, finding and expressing your authentic voice becomes a powerful act of liberation. Whether through conversation, creative expression, or advocacy, speaking your truth can deepen your sense of identity and connection. It reaffirms that your experiences matter, your feelings are valid, and you deserve to be heard.

One thing to keep in mind is that healing doesn't mean forgetting or pretending the trauma never happened. Instead, it's about reclaiming your narrative with compassion and courage. Your story winds through pain and hope, struggle and triumph, shadow and light. Embracing the full complexity of this journey builds resilience and offers a profound kind of freedom that transcends old wounds.

Remember too that emotional freedom opens a doorway to living a richer, more intentional life. It lets you prioritize joy, peace, creativity, and connection rather than merely managing distress or numbing discomfort. This expanded way of being invites you to build relationships and experiences that honor your growth and support your well-being. Ultimately, it's about creating a life you feel proud of and deeply connected to—one where your past shapes you but no longer confines you.

The path ahead will continue to unfold in unexpected ways, with moments of clarity and moments that test your resolve. By believing in your capacity to heal, by practicing self-compassion, and by surrounding yourself with support, you lay down the roots for a freedom that endures. You are worthy of this transformation, and your story of healing has the power to inspire not only yourself but those around you.

As you close this chapter of your journey, take a moment to celebrate how far you've come. Each act of self-kindness, every boundary you've set, each tear you've allowed yourself to shed, has brought you closer to the peace you seek. Walking this path is no small feat. May you carry forward with hope in your heart, strength in your step, and openness to the endless possibilities that lie ahead.

APPENDIX: RESOURCES FOR CONTINUED SUPPORT AND GROWTH

The journey toward healing from childhood trauma doesn't end when you close this book; in many ways, that's just the beginning. Growth and recovery are ongoing processes that unfold over time, often with the help of external support and trusted resources. This appendix is designed to guide you to places, communities, and tools that can keep you inspired, informed, and grounded as you continue working toward lasting emotional freedom.

Finding resources that resonate with your unique experience can deepen your healing and offer practical guidance when challenges arise. Whether you're someone navigating your own path, a mental health professional supporting others, or a loved one learning how to provide compassionate care, having a reliable toolbox makes all the difference.

Where to Find Professional Support

Therapy often serves as a cornerstone in trauma recovery. Licensed counselors, psychologists, and trauma specialists provide safe spaces to explore painful memories and develop new coping skills. If finding the right therapist feels overwhelming, consider organizations that offer directories or referrals tailored to trauma-informed care. Many professionals also offer teletherapy options, increasing accessibility no matter where you live.

Support Groups and Community Connections

Healing isn't meant to happen in isolation. Support groups create environments where sharing experiences helps reduce feelings of shame or loneliness. They connect you with others who truly understand the complex emotions tied to childhood trauma. Look for groups facilitated by trained leaders—either in person or online—that foster confidentiality and emotional safety.

Educational Books, Podcasts, and Online Courses

Diving deeper into trauma's effects and recovery methods can empower you to take control of your healing journey. Select resources from trusted experts that offer evidence-based approaches without overwhelming jargon. Whether you prefer reading, listening to podcasts during a walk, or engaging in interactive online workshops, there's something to meet every learning style and pace.

Self-Care and Mindfulness Tools

Integrating self-care practices into daily life strengthens resilience and builds emotional regulation. Resources that teach mindfulness, grounding techniques, and somatic awareness are particularly valuable. You might explore guided meditation apps, journaling prompts, or creative outlets like art therapy, each offering different pathways to reconnect with your body and mind.

Advocacy and Awareness Organizations

Many nonprofit organizations focus on raising awareness about childhood trauma and its long-term impact. Engaging with or supporting these groups can provide not only valuable information but also a sense of purpose and community. By participating, you contribute to breaking the stigma and expanding understanding within society.

Keep in mind that the right resources for you may evolve over time as your needs and strengths change. Stay curious, gentle, and patient with yourself as you explore what helps move you closer to healing and wholeness. Growth often takes unexpected turns, but with the right support, it becomes a journey filled with hope and possibility.

* 9 7 8 1 9 1 8 2 2 3 2 5 5 *